Defying the Odds

Defying the Odds

An Independent Senator's Historic Campaign

by

Harry F. Byrd Jr.

United States Senator

1965-1983

ACKNOWLEDGEMENTS

There is a lot more to book publishing than just writing
the book. I learned that the hard way with the help of
many, especially Charles Bartlett, Edward Grimsley,
Wynnona Kirk, Richard R. J. Morin, Barbara Byrd and
Karel McClellan.

ISBN 0-9666870-0-0

Library of Congress Catalog Card No. 98-061532

Printed by RR Donnelley & Sons Company
Harrisonburg, Virginia

In memory of

Gretchen —

and our 48 happy years.

PREFACE

Even with the hindsight of almost three decades, the 1970 decision by Virginia's Democratic U. S. Senator Harry F. Byrd Jr. to run for reelection as an Independent strikes an observer as breathtakingly original and tremendously gutsy. Few politicians then or now would risk everything on an electoral gamble that is almost without precedent. Close friends counseled against it. Colleagues pronounced it foolhardy. Some in Senator Byrd's old party felt betrayed, yet many members of the other major party were unwilling to embrace a man clearly intent on blazing his own singular trail. The incumbent president, Richard Nixon, was rebuffed, his blandishments turned aside. No party money or well-oiled partisan machinery would be available for a difficult campaign. Adding all this together, one is astounded that a seasoned, highly successful politician such as Senator Byrd would do such a thing.

But do it he did. In so doing, Senator Byrd made American history, becoming only the second U. S. Senator to be elected as an Independent [1]. (When Mr. Byrd won again in 1976, he became the first Independent ever re-elected to the Senate.) Moreover,

---

[1] Republican U.S. Senator George Norris of Nebraska preceded Mr. Byrd in 1936, winning a new term as an Independent.

and most impressively, he took on both a Democratic nominee <u>and</u> a Republican nominee, yet won an <u>absolute majority</u> of the votes cast (53.5 percent of the over 900,000 ballots). Senator Byrd captured rural Virginia, the suburbs, and even the liberal central cities. A mere 13 counties and three cities, most of these in the party-oriented "Fightin' Ninth" congressional district, eluded his grasp.

Political scientists, who had been taught from Government 101 onwards that the voters' party loyalties make it nearly impossible for Independents to win, were sent scurrying back to their classrooms and desks to revise lectures and texts. The political parties themselves, in Virginia and elsewhere, were taught some valuable lessons, too - not least that party loyalty can sometimes demand too much of a free people.

With an unassuming manner and economic prose, Senator Byrd makes just this point in the pages that follow. While he does not boast at all about his overwhelming victory, he would certainly be entitled to do so. The truth is, just about everyone on the political scene in 1970 — friend and foe — was wrong about the results of his decision. How did Senator Byrd so calmly and deliberately choose a highly unorthodox path to power? The Senator tells us this fascinating tale, conjuring up great ghosts from a dramatic era of change.

To this analyst, it all really came down to Senator Byrd's ability to stick to his principles. Senator Byrd objected to the Democratic Party's loyalty oath and increasing liberalism, so he simply could not run again as a Democrat. He also did not feel comfortable becoming a Republican, a move that would have forced him to abandon some close friends and yield his seniority in the Senate. Since he wanted to continue in public service, only one option remained, that of Independency, however hazardous it might be to his political future.

Senator Byrd sensed that if he carefully explained the reasons for his decision, the people of Virginia would rally to him. He worked hard on his announcement (reprinted in its entirety later in this volume), and evidently the voters did understand and respect it. Legions of Democrats and Republicans rushed to Senator Byrd's banner, so that the 1970 contest was never really in doubt at any point in the general election campaign. But when Senator Byrd first filed as an Independent, there were many (including *Time* magazine) who were ready to write his political obituary. Like Mark Twain, the reports of Senator Byrd's death were greatly exaggerated.

Significantly, too, Senator Byrd's leap into the unknown had unforeseen consequences of great moment. Party realignment in Virginia and the South was aided by the Byrd candidacy. Conservatives left the Democratic Party in droves in 1970, never to return. In addition, Senator Byrd legitimized "independent" status for voters of both parties, encouraging the loosening of party ties and the popular predisposition to vote "for the person, not the party." Undoubtedly, Senator Byrd's solid reelection made it easier for his good friend, former Governor Mills E. Godwin, Jr., to run for a second term as governor in 1973. The senator's big victory also helped to move the Virginia Republican party to the right, so that a united coalition of conservatives could find a new home and once again dominate politics in a conservative state.

Most of all, Senator Byrd's election as an Independent stands even today as both a model and a warning. It is a model for politicians who feel shut out by the two major parties and wish to find an alternative route to office. And it is a warning to the two major political parties that their duopoly is not invincible, that under the right set of circumstances, a special individual can manage to confound conventional wisdom and deliver a message to the political establishment — just as Harry F. Byrd, Jr., did on that momentous election day twenty-eight years ago.

Dr. Larry J. Sabato
Professor of Government and Foreign Affairs
University of Virginia

INTRODUCTION

First, I suppose, I should identify my political philosophy.

If one believes that Thomas Jefferson's philosophy was a liberal one, and historically it has been so construed, then I should be considered a liberal.

Like Jefferson, I fear centralization of power; I feel that the least governed are the best governed; I am not convinced that Washington, D.C. knows best how the local problems of the 3,097 counties of the United States should be solved; and most certainly I agree with Jefferson that the greatest danger to a democracy is overspending by the representatives of the people.

But today's liberal advocates courses precisely the opposite from those cited above. Today's liberal favors greater federal power, believes that Washington, D.C. knows best how our local school systems and other local problems should be handled; and favors more spending and more taxes.

By today's definition, most certainly I am not a liberal; thus it follows that I must be a conservative.

Conservatism comes from the same root as conservation: I believe in conservation of fundamental principles, of natural resources, of human dignity, and the conservation of the taxpayer's hard earned dollar.

A deep mistrust of governmental power is a re-

current theme in early American history.   James
Madison, a chief architect of our Federal system declared: "All men having power ought to be mistrusted."

Thomas Jefferson put it even stronger. In a state-
ment which I feel should be graven in stone in the
Senate of the United States, the House of
Representatives, the Supreme Court and the Oval
Office of the White House, Jefferson declared:

> "In questions of power, let no more be heard
> of confidence in man, but bind him down from
> mischief by the chains of the Constitution."

Those men who signed the Declaration of
Independence, those who fought the American
Revolution, those who put together and then ratified the
Constitution of the United States, had lived under op-
pression.

Through their own experience, they forged the
fundamentals of American democracy designed to pro-
tect individuals from government tyranny.

Harry F. Byrd Jr.
U.S . Senator
1965-1983

Chapter 1

****

Regardless of how many times one has attended White House dinners, they are always impressive. Occasionally they are too stiff, and too formal, but such was not the case on the evening of June 4, 1968.

The President and I were one seat apart. Between us was the wife of the guest of honor, a South American president. She spoke only Spanish. So the President and I spent most of the dinner talking with each other. We were long-time friends and had much in common, but not always on the same page politically.

Toward the end of the dinner, Lyndon B. Johnson leaned closer to me and said, "Harry, I will be out of office in seven months - but before I leave I want to do something for you. What do you want?"

I said, "I am grateful to you, Mr. President, and grateful for your friendship, but there is nothing I want."

President Johnson, not accustomed to taking NO

for an answer, followed by saying "What about a judge-ship." I replied that I had recommended someone for the federal vacancy in Virginia, saying he is an excellent lawyer with judicial temperament, his name is . . . the President put up his hand "I don't care about his name, if you want him, then I want him."

"Here is what you do," he continued, "call my Attorney General (Ramsey Clark). He isn't worth a damn, but tell him I want your man appointed." I thanked the President.

At 3 o'clock the next morning the phone rang at my Washington residence; it was my close friend, D. Lathan Mims, who gave me the news that Senator Robert Kennedy had been shot and killed in California. Kennedy was seeking the Democratic presidential nomination. This tragic event threw all of Washington into turmoil, especially the Justice Department. I reasoned it was not the time to be talking with the Attorney General about a judgeship.

I let time pass and then called one of the president's assistants. I told him of the dinner conversation, asked him to check the accuracy of my statement with the President, and suggested it would be best if The White House were to tell the Attorney General of the president's wishes in regard to the judgeship. The White House phoned later to say all of this had been done.

On June 26 another event occurred: President

Johnson nominated Abe Fortas, then an Associate Justice, to be Chief Justice of the United States which, of course, required Senate confirmation. This, I immediately recognized, put me on the hot spot in regard to the federal judgeship in Virginia.

I had hoped I could vote for the Fortas nomination for many reasons, among which were my desire to give support to Lyndon Johnson; my feeling it would be appreciated in the Jewish community, for which I had a high regard and which consistently had given me good support; and, thirdly, I felt it could help stem the loss of support among Democratic activists feeling unhappy about some of my votes.

Lyndon B. Johnson

A yes vote on Fortas, I thought, could be a political plus.

I set about to study his judicial record. But the more I studied it, the more concerned I became.

After giving it much thought, I reached the conclusion I could not cast my vote to confirm Fortas; and, in addition, I felt I must make a carefully prepared Senate speech making clear my reasons.

I telephoned Alex Harman of Pulaski, my nominee for the federal judgeship in Virginia, and told him what I felt I had to do, and if I did make such a speech it would jeopardize if not kill his appointment.

I appreciated and never forgot Alex's reply: "I would like to be a federal judge, and believe I would be a good one. But if you believe the confirmation of Fortas as Chief Justice of the United States would not be in the best interests of our country, I accept your decision. My disappointment is not adequate reason to go against your best judgment on a matter of such great importance."

(Several years later, my long-time friend, Governor Mills E. Godwin Jr., appointed Alex to the Supreme Court of Virginia).

Chapter 2

✳✳✳✳

I spoke in the Senate on September 9, 1968, three months and five days after The White House dinner. It was a lengthy speech. I felt the Senate had a deep obligation to go carefully into the Fortas record as an associate justice. Once a nominee is confirmed by the Senate, assuming the nominee's good behavior, there are no checks or restraints on his lifetime appointment. Fortas had been confirmed as Associate Justice by voice vote without opposition.

As an Associate Justice, Mr. Fortas became a key player in what I regarded as the excesses of the Court under Earl Warren as Chief Justice.

The nomination of Mr. Justice Fortas was submitted on June 26. Many of my colleagues argued that because President Johnson announced on March 31 that he would not be a candidate for reelection, he therefore, was a "lame duck" President and should not submit nominations for the Federal Judiciary.

I did not agree with such a view.

Every President continues to have the power and the responsibilities of his office until the hour he relinquishes it to his successor. John Marshall, perhaps the most famous of all the top justices, was appointed only days before John Adams relinquished the Presidency to Thomas Jefferson, a political opponent of Marshall.

When does a President become a "lame duck" insofar as submitting nominations is concerned? Seven months before he leaves office, 14 months, or four years? Bear in mind that the Constitution now prevents a President from serving more than two terms. So any President who begins his second term automatically is barred from seeking reelection.

I put little credence in the arguments of those who said that President Johnson should not, seven months before the end of his term, submit a nomination for the Supreme Court.

The Senate's responsibility, as I saw it, "is to meet the issue head on, to deal squarely with the qualifications and the philosophy of the appointee ...."

In my Senate speech, I quoted liberally from various Supreme Court Justices. I expressed the view that appointees should possess the qualities of justices like Oliver Wendell Holmes, Louis D. Brandeis, Charles Evans Hughes, Harlan Fiske Stone, Benjamin H. Cardozo, and Felix Frankfurter.

I reflected the view of Mr. Justice Cardozo that

"justices are not commissioned to make and unmake rules at pleasure, in accordance with changing views of expediency or wisdom." I maintained that a majority of the Warren Court had consistently done precisely this.

I quoted Mr. Justice Frankfurter, who contended that the court should not repudiate "the experience of our whole past in asserting destructively novel judicial power."

Earlier Mr. Justice Frankfurter warned against such action:

"The court's authority - possessed of neither the purse nor the sword - ultimately rests on sustained public confidence in its moral sanction. Such feeling must be nourished by the Court's complete detachment . . . from political entanglements ..."

In my speech to the Senate, I said the Supreme Court needed to be brought into balance, that under Mr. Warren it had become an extremist court; a majority, which usually included Mr. Fortas, had taken the court to the far left.

I concluded my speech with an unequivocal summary of my objection to the nominee:

"During the time Mr. Fortas has been a member of this Court, he has established himself as a disciple of Chief Justice Warren and has embraced wholeheartedly the Warren philosophy.

"If I were to vote to elevate him to the position of Chief Justice, I would be voting to give him the authority to influence decisions by assigning cases to other justices to write opinions; and the authority to assign judges and retired judges to circuit and district courts throughout the nation.

"If I were to support the confirmation of Mr. Justice Fortas to the position of Chief Justice, I would be voting to promote a member of the Court who had embraced, and become a part of, the Warren philosophy - a philosophy that decrees that the Court may cast legal precedent aside when it does not square with personal desires of the judges.

"If I were to cast my vote for Mr. Justice Fortas, I would be placing my stamp of approval on the extreme leftist trend of the Warren court, a trend to which Mr. Justice Fortas apparently has dedicated himself....

"Were I to vote to ratify the nomination of Mr. Justice Fortas to be Chief Justice, I would be voting to perpetuate, in the key judicial position in our nation, the Warren philosophy.

"As one who feels the Warren court has done great damage to our nation - to the future welfare of our people - how can I vote to confirm as Chief Justice one who proclaims the Warren era the greatest in Court history; not only proclaims it in words, but by deeds, namely, by his decisions as Associate Justice?

"That Mr. Warren and Mr. Fortas were determined to perpetuate the centralization of power in Washington was dramatized by Chief Justice Warren's statement in press interviews that if the nomination of Mr. Fortas was not confirmed, he, Mr. Warren would continue to serve."

I pointed out that by thus conditioning his retirement, Mr. Warren was telling the Senate. "either you take my preference as a successor or I won't retire." I suggested that the Senate would not want to be so coerced.

Senate opposition intensified with each passing day and Fortas' nomination was withdrawn October 4, 1968. Johnson, Fortas and Warren had lost the battle. That ended the President's interest in the federal judgeship in Virginia.

I debated with myself whether to talk with the President again regarding Alex Harmon. I decided to do so 30 days before Johnson's term expired, because it was Johnson who had volunteered support for my nominee.

I was cordially received by the President when we met in the Oval Office.

As we sat down the President started talking, looking around the room as if he were talking to himself: "I don't understand the Senate. I served there and was majority leader but I still don't get it. Abe Fortas would have made a great chief justice. I don't get it, I don't understand the Senate."

Then abruptly he turned his attention to me and said, "What is it you want to talk with me about?"

Of course, he knew the answer to that question; and of course `I did not comment on his ruminations about the Senate and Fortas.

I recalled for him our dinner conversation of the past June.

He quickly replied: "Of course, I remember our conversation. The problem is the Attorney General and your Virginia colleague (William Spong of Portsmouth) want someone else. I want your man."

My reply was brief: "If you are with me, Mr. President, it doesn't make much difference who the Attorney General wants or who Spong wants."

Then he jumped out of his chair and said "follow me." With a quick walk to the next office he spoke loudly to his assistant:

"You telephone my Attorney General and tell him I want Senator Byrd's man appointed to the Virginia judgeship."

I thanked him, we shook hands and said goodbye.

I was not however surprised that nothing subsequently happened. The federal judgeship in Virginia remained vacant.

The Fortas nomination and my part in it was one of various political events that led to what became Virginia's politically historic year of 1970, which this book is all about.

It was in 1968, too, that another event tore at the seams of the Democratic Party.

Democrat Mills E. Godwin Jr. in 1965 had defeated Republican Linwood Holton for Governor by a huge majority. Mills had been a dynamic and popular governor.

But at the Democratic State Convention in Roanoke in 1968, the liberal element of the Democratic party began to flex its muscle. The liberals attempted to oust Virginia's Democratic Chairman, Congressman Watkins Abbitt of the fourth district. He narrowly won reelection, defeating liberal Joe Fitzpatrick of Norfolk.

Governor Godwin strongly supported Abbitt, as did I. In the fight to succeed retiring Democratic National Committeeman Sidney Kellam, Godwin and I both supported Waldo Miles of Bristol. After a bitter battle, Miles was defeated by State Senator William B. Hopkins of Roanoke.

When Governor Godwin addressed the convention, many liberals actually jeered the Democratic governor. At this many of us became alarmed because it was clear that the liberal forces were determined to take over the leadership of the party.

Chapter 3

✳✳✳✳

I knew that many Democrats were not happy with what some regarded as my inadequate support for the Democratic president. My speech against the Senate confirmation of Abe Fortas added fuel to a smoldering fire, as did my lack of enthusiasm for the 1968 presidential nominee, Vice President Hubert Humphrey.

In late December of 1969 and early January of 1970, my wife Gretchen and I spent 10 days alone on a Caribbean island. I told Gretchen that the two of us must develop a response and a strategy if the Democratic Committee attempted to discipline me.

I felt in my "political bones" that the committee would take some punitive action, but had no idea what it might be. I rehashed the possibilities with Gretchen so much during those 10 days that I could sense that I had begun to bore her.

I took with me to the island a biography of George W. Norris, a Republican senator from Nebraska, up for reelection in 1936. Norris was fifth in seniority in the Senate. He was a liberal Republican who had decided to support the reelection of Democrat Franklin D. Roosevelt.   Norris announced he would seek reelection to the Senate as an Independent. The Republicans nominated a candidate against him, as did the Democrats. Norris won with 45% of the vote.

The Norris precedent, I thought, might be a possibility for me. If the liberal Democrats pressed me to the wall, I could find myself forced to take a dangerous and unprecedented step.

Shortly after we returned from the Caribbean, I decided to test the Norris precedent with my close friend, former Governor William M. Tuck.

Gov. William M. Tuck

But, first I needed a place to meet; I didn't want a hotel. So, I called my dear friend Tennant Bryan in Richmond - he was publisher of the two Richmond newspapers - and asked him if I could use his home for a confidential meeting with former Governor Tuck. He invited me to spend the night and suggested Bill Tuck come to the Bryan home the next morning after he

(Tennant) had gone to work.

William M. Tuck had been a member of the Virginia House of Delegates; State Senator, Lieutenant Governor, Governor and had just retired after 14 years in the House of Representatives in Washington. He knew Virginia well - all of Virginia - and was one of my closest friends.

Bill and I talked for nearly three hours. When I threw out my idea of running as an Independent, he was doubtful. He seemed confident that I could win the primary.

But as we talked and debated the pros and cons of an Independent run, Bill began to show enthusiasm. As we wound up our meeting, I had the impression that he agreed with me that my idea was sound.

But several days later, I got a four-page letter from Bill in which he strongly advised against it. The letter was handwritten and difficult to read, but its main point was clear: The risks of an independent run are too great and "it would be best for you to seek the Democratic nomination." He promised however to give full support to whatever decision I made.

I decided to remain flexible and await developments.

The "development" came on the afternoon of the annual Democratic Jefferson-Jackson dinner, always held in Richmond at the John Marshall Hotel. In 1970, the date was Saturday, February 21.

Persons at the dinner seemed unaware of any significant resolutions adopted by the Democratic Central Committee that afternoon. I made a few discreet inquiries but everything appeared to have been routine.

When the head table of the two Senators, the Congressmen, the Lieutenant Governor and the Attorney General were individually introduced, I received a very satisfying ovation.

The Associated Press reported, "it appeared Byrd received the biggest ovation at the dinner." That was encouraging; my staff had told me a public opinion poll indicated I would have difficulty winning a Democratic primary.

The next morning the newspapers headlined the most important resolution adopted by the State Central Committee, but most of us did not immediately recognize the potential impact. It took me a good 48 hours to realize the full significance of the committee's decision to impose a loyalty obligation on every Democratic candidate in Virginia elections.

Here is *The Associated Press* lead paragraph written by veteran political reporter John Daffron:

> RICHMOND (AP)- The Virginia Democratic Party agreed yesterday to require candidates for office to pledge support of all Democratic nominees from the Court House to the White House.

I belatedly came to understand just how serious had become my political problem; the first thing I said to myself "What do I do now?"

I already knew Governor Tuck's view, and his deep concern about an Independent run. What are my options? With whom can I consult? My only firm conclusion was to say nothing, give no indication of concern.

I needed to consult, but with whom?

I felt there were two criteria: those who knew the entire state; many knew regions but very few had a good grasp of the politics of Virginia as a whole.

The second need was even more difficult to find than the first: persons I

Gov. Albertis Harrison

could trust to keep the matter in strict confidence; the two criteria must be in one person - and it's a rare politician who has much regard for confidentiality.

My two closest friends in the Virginia Senate were Albertis Harrison and Mills Godwin. I couldn't discuss it with Mills because it would put him in an untenable position; as the outgoing Democratic Governor he was considered the head of the party.

Former Governor Harrison had been appointed to

the Supreme Court of Virginia, so he was not available for political consultation. Nevertheless, I had an obligation to talk with him, as he had appointed me to the Senate five years earlier.

I told him by telephone that I was considering seeking reelection as an Independent. He said he would not try to dissuade me because he agreed that the Democratic Party had departed from some of the principles we both had long cherished. Whatever I decided, he said, would be satisfactory to him.

I got the firm impression that only judicial restraint kept him from saying, "Right on, Harry." I was encouraged.

M. J. Menefee, my father's long-time administrative assistant, and mine for my first year in the Senate, was cool to an Independent run. "Peachy" Menefee was a keen politician who had been elected to local office, and after a long service with my father, he knew Virginia well. He didn't say no to my suggestion but he was reluctant to say yes because he suspected I could not win without party support.

Like Bill Tuck, he expressed much concern as to the attitude of local Democratic office-holders; the Sheriffs, the Commissioners of Revenue, the county-city Treasurers, the Commonwealth Attorneys, the Clerks of Court - all influential in politics.

I had less concern because I had observed that, generally speaking, most local office-holders are not leaders - they tend to follow the prevailing local senti-ment.

I believed that if I showed strength in a particular community, the local elected officials would stay silent or give me quiet support; if my support in their community was weak, they would be likely to turn against me. I was willing to take the risk.

D. Lathan Mims

As a member of the Virginia Senate, I had worked closely with Ben Lacy, then Clerk of the state Senate. He had a sensitive feel for politics. He knew Virginia well and was about as close-mouthed as anybody I knew. He liked the idea as soon as I conveyed it to him. He was enthusiastic because he thought that it would work.

My most detailed discussions were with my close friend and newspaper associate, D. Lathan Mims, editor and general manager of *The Daily News-Record,* a Byrd newspaper in Harrisonburg.

Lathan was admirable in every way. A native of South Carolina, he had been a Colonel in the U. S. Army during World War II, then news editor for *The Associated Press* in the two Carolinas. He had been with me for 15 years. He was a man of solid judgment and total integrity.

He was intrigued with the possibility of my independent stance, but like others, he was uncertain that I could win without the organizational support of a political party. He kept telling me he was not a politician as he acknowledged his fear of an Independent run.

I felt it important also to consult with two Senate colleagues: Richard B. Russell of Georgia and Russell B. Long of Louisiana.

Dick Russell was the senior member of the Senate, after holding his seat for 37 years. Dick and my father came to the Senate the same year and they were close friends. I had known him through those years; he was my closest friend when I went to the U. S. Senate, after 18 years in the Virginia Senate.

Of the many fine Senators with whom I have served, I would put none ahead of Dick Russell. He had it all - courage, fine judgment, integrity. His life was politics. He became Governor of Georgia in his early thirties. He also was chairman of one of the committees to which I was assigned, Armed Services. I valued his judgment.

He listened carefully as I recited the background of the challenge facing me. After hearing my story, Dick said he wanted to see me reelected regardless of how I ran, but said he didn't feel he had adequate knowledge of Virginia politics to advise me on the best course. I said that I nevertheless wanted to hear his views on the pros and cons of an Independent course.

As we talked, Dick began to show enthusiasm for an Independent run; he said he saw merit to my thinking. We agreed to meet again the following week but at that time he had become cautious like Bill Tuck. He had decided it was so risky that he couldn't recommend taking the chance.

But Dick made one point which stayed in my mind: Running as an Independent, I would draw votes from both political parties, leaving the nominee of both parties without a unified base.

Next, I met with Russell Long of Louisiana, whom I regarded as having probably the best political mind in the Senate. Russell Long and I are about the same age and we were close friends. He was chairman of the Senate Finance Committee on which I served.

As I outlined my situation, his response was prompt, brief and enthusiastic: "Do it", he said. He then outlined some factors that I hadn't even considered.

He recalled that my first election in 1966, had been close (8200 vote majority) because the chief issue against me was the creation of a dynasty, as I was seeking to succeed my father. (In the long history of the Senate, up to this year of 1998, only two senators ever have been elected as the *direct* successors to their fathers, Robert M. LaFollette Jr. of Wisconsin in 1926 and myself in 1966). Long said that in cutting my ties to the party which my father once headed, I would show a boldness and a willingness to go it alone on serious matters of principle. His enthusiasm grew as he spoke, and I must admit that my pulse quickened.

Chapter 4

※※※※

The political clock was running; the deadline for a decision was near. A saying that I sometimes quote came to mind: "a little less chatter and a lot more action, it's time for the main attraction."

For me the main attraction was a "decision"; and now that I could no longer procrastinate, the "decision" seemed easy. Unwilling to sign the pledge demanded by the Democratic Party, I could not seek the Democratic nomination. Ergo, I run as an Independent.

I still had not given any hint as to what I might do. I only discussed the planning that had to be done with Lathan Mims.

I set Tuesday, March 17 as the date on which I would make the statewide television address to the Virginia people. That date was earlier than was legally necessary; the filing deadline for the Democratic primary was April 15. I felt a sentimental need to give the Democratic Party adequate time to react to my inten-

22

tions. After all, I had won public office seven times as a Democrat.

Having set the date for the public announcement, I put aside time to write a speech to the Virginia people to make clear my reasons. I wrote it in longhand, revising it as I went along. In fact, I revised it a number of times even after I had thought I had finished.

In attempting to do what no person in Virginia had ever done - and only one person in the entire United States had succeeded in doing - I felt that every word must be weighed carefully to avoid any implications that could be used against me by my opponents. I had to anticipate opposition from both parties so my speech to Virginia voters must be clear, firm and precise.

My next step was to fly alone to a television studio in North Carolina (I wouldn't chance a leak from a Virginia station).

After delivering my speech to tape, I had copies made for delivery to every television station in the State of Virginia. The release time was 6 p.m. Tuesday, March 17.

I wrote a telegram that would be sent early Monday morning to many Democratic friends - persons with whom I had worked closely in campaigns through the years.

The text of the telegram read: "After a great deal of thought I have decided on a new approach which some people perhaps will regard as a bold one. I hope you will approve. I have just finalized a statement I am making Tuesday night and am mailing you a copy."

By Friday evening I turned everything over to Lathan Mims and Jack F. Davis, editor and general manager of my Winchester newspaper. They said the tapes should not be delivered before mid-afternoon Tuesday. They spent the weekend developing a plan to do just that and to convey the text of my speech to every newspaper.

Gov. Mills E. Godwin

Now, my solitary work was done. Lathan and Jack would carry the ball; I sat back, confident that they were reaching out to friends across the state.

That was the Friday before Tuesday March 17. There was still one close personal and political friend I wanted to see, the head of the party I was about to leave. But it was a different party now, one which he himself would shortly abandon.

I phoned Mills Godwin and asked if he would meet me at the Norfolk Airport Monday morning. I said I was flying back to Washington immediately after our meeting.

Saturday night was the annual Gridiron Dinner, an organization of Washington correspondents of newspapers throughout the United States. The President (Nixon) was there, and when I spoke with him he said "Harry, it's time you and I get together again."

I knew what that meant; he wanted me to run for reelection as a Republican. I replied, "Fine, Mr. President, let me know when."

Early Monday morning The White House called to ask that I meet with the President that day. I knew if I did that, it would compromise my Tuesday plans. I asked the President's assistant to thank the President but tell him I did not think this would be an appropriate time; I added, "I think he will understand."

My Monday meeting with Mills was cordial. I knew the delicacy of his situation. As the outgoing Democratic Governor, he was regarded as the titular head of the Party. I did not want to put him on the spot. I told him I was not asking for support or commitment, but just wanted to tell him in person what I was planning to do.

Mills said he could not make a commitment - except to say he would not run against me.

After my television speech Mills made a statement to the press in which he expressed "regret" over my move and added "I would not attempt at this time to pass judgment on this decision."

Chapter 5

✳✳✳✳

Following is the speech in which I revealed and explained my decision to the people of Virginia, March 17, 1970:

My dear fellow Virginians,

I would like to think out loud with those whom I have the high honor - and the great responsibility - to represent in the Senate of the United States.

I love Virginia. I love every area of Virginia - every mountain, every valley, every seashore. And I love her people.

Our people are, I feel, forward looking, responsible and moderate. We realize, too, that those of us representing the public must be attuned to the 1970s. We realize that times and conditions change - but that fundamental principles do not.

As you know, I have spent most of my adult life serving the people of Virginia to the best of my capabilities. For 18 years I served in the Senate of Virginia. I am now in my fifth year in the Senate of the United States.

During the past four sessions of the Congress, I have cast more than 1,000 recorded votes. My votes, my speeches, my views are a matter of record. This is available to all.

I cannot change that record. I would not change it if I could. I realize that no one will agree with every vote, but in each of them I have voted my convictions.

I have fought for the programs of the President - Democrat or Republican - when I thought he was right. I have fought against the programs of the President - Democrat or Republican - when I thought he was wrong.

I have acted independently of party lines. But I feel I have acted in the best interests of Virginia and of our nation. I have maintained that independence because I believe Virginians are independent, free - thinking people.

My term as United States Senator expires next January. This coming November, Virginians will vote to determine whom they wish to represent them in the United States Senate for the following six years.

I have given considerable thought as to how I can best submit my record to the voters of Virginia for their approval or disapproval.

The problems which face our nation are immense - both at home and abroad. The war. Inflation. Civil

Unrest. Crime. Pollution of air and water. Unrestrained government spending. Heavy taxation.

There is no Democratic solution to these problems; there is no Republican solution.

Party labels mean less and less to Virginians - and, indeed, to most Americans. They know that it is principle, rather than labels, upon which this nation was built.

In this modern age, more and more Virginians are thinking in terms of the general election. Fewer and fewer are participating in primaries. The best evidence of this was last year's gubernatorial primary. It drew fewer than one-fourth of the qualified voters.

Another important factor must be taken into consideration.

During 1969, the various candidates for Governor spent a total of $3 million. This is a staggering sum. Never before in Virginia have such huge sums been spent to achieve public office.

This is a deplorable trend. It discourages many from seeking public office. It could lead to undue influence.

Virginia, long noted for its integrity in high office, must not go the way of other states where elections are decided by wild spending.

Obviously, two election campaigns - a Primary followed by a General Election - would be twice as expensive as one campaign. Is this in the best interests of the people of Virginia?

I have listed two factors in my thinking.

Now we come to the most important.

Last month the Democratic State Central Committee took an unprecedented step. For the first time in 40 years, a Virginia Senator, if he is to seek re-election in the Democratic Primary, will be required to sign an oath that he will support for President whoever is selected by the Democratic National Convention.

Veteran political writer John F. Daffron reported for The Associated Press the actions of the committee in these words:

> *"RICHMOND (AP) - The Virginia Democratic Party agreed yesterday to require candidates for office to pledge support of all Democratic nominees from the courthouse to the White House."*

The Committee is within its rights to require such an oath. I do not contest its action.

But this action has made it impossible for me to file in the Democratic Primary.

I cannot, and will not, sign an oath to vote for and support an individual whose identity I do not know and whose principles and policies are thus unknown.

To sign such a blank check would be, I feel, the height of irresponsibility and unworthy of a member of the United States Senate.

I have given this matter a great deal of thought since the Committee action three weeks ago.

I am told that I could sign such an oath and forget it.

Perhaps there is a technicality behind which I could hide, but the intent of the Committee requirement is clear.

Whatever I do, I want to do in good faith.

One reason Americans, and especially our young people, have become cynical about persons in public life is because too many politicians have become cynical, saying one thing prior to election and feeling free to do something else after election.

No one knows today who will be the Democratic nominee for President in 1972 - nor who will be the Republican nominee. No one knows what philosophy they will advocate.

The year 1972 will be a crucial one for our nation.

Before making a decision as to whom I shall support for President, I want to know the alternatives - and just where each candidate stands on the dominant issues.

To forfeit now my right to do this is to me unthinkable.

I had thought that this matter of a loyalty oath had been settled 18 years ago when Virginia's Governor

John S. Battle told the 1952 Democratic National Convention in these words . . . "We in Virginia are not going to sign any pledge or any commitment which will prevent freedom of thought and freedom of action."

Governor Battle made this statement in the convention four days before a presidential candidate was chosen. I would be required to subscribe to an oath two years before a candidate is chosen.

I am anxious to serve the people of Virginia in the United States Senate. I love our country, and I feel I can continue to make a contribution to Virginia and to the nation as a United States Senator.

Occasionally there comes a time when one must break with precedent, when one must do the unusual.

For me, such a time has come.

I shall take a fresh approach - to some, perhaps, a bold approach.

At this particular time - in this particular situation - in this particular election - I feel I can best serve Virginia by taking my record directly to all of the people in Virginia in November.

Now is not the time - it is too early - to announce my candidacy for the Senate. But being an independent Democrat I shall, at the appropriate time, file as an Independent in order to preserve my freedom of action.

I realize full well the difficulties I face in this decision. The course I am taking is an uncharted one.

But I would rather be a free man than a captive

Senator.

*I want and need the support of all Virginians -
Democrats, Republicans, Independents.*

*At a later date - between now and November - I
shall discuss in detail my Senate record, and I shall
continue to make known my views on the great issues
facing our nation.*

*I have been independent in casting my votes in
Washington, and I shall take only one oath - and that to
the people of Virginia: To conscientiously and impar-
tially serve all the people of our great state.*

Chapter 6

There is no doubt that the state was taken by surprise. The early reaction was muted, but it heated up quickly and on Wednesday, my office was bombarded by the news media. I kept out of sight and refused all requests for interviews. I remember Jack Davis, who almost always kept his cool, got quite annoyed with me for refusing a press conference.

I said tell the news media I will have a full scale press conference at the John Marshall Hotel in Richmond at 2 p.m. Thursday, but not before. Jack was not happy that I put it off that long - four news cycles after the original announcement. But I wanted my reasons to sink in before new quotes from me could be obtained.

I loved that news conference. My statement to the Virginia people had not attacked anyone. In fact, I had asserted that the Democratic Central Committee was within its rights to require the pledge; I did not ask that the pledge be rescinded.

Since it was difficult to attack my speech, the focus was kept where I wanted it. The committee had the right to require the pledge - and I had the right to refuse. I answered questions for 35 minutes.

Among the questions: Did I plan to start a third political party?

Answer: "NO. The decision I was forced to make is a personal one; it involved no one else.

"It is a decision for this particular time, this particular election, this particular situation.

"Whether it's the politically wise decision can only be determined in November, but I believe it's the right decision.

"I hope my Senate record will have the support of a majority of Democrats, a majority of Republicans, a majority of Independents."

Question: Would your father have signed the loyalty oath?

Answer: "No, I don't think so. But the difference is this: he would have made the decision in 24 hours. It took me three weeks."

But, what made the news conference so much fun for me - and which, I thought, made several important points for my benefit - was a *Washington Post* editorial that morning. *The Post* castigated me for my course of action.

I took *The Post* editorial with me and held it up

and read the two key points, namely, Byrd's action made it impossible for Virginia's fine new Republican governor - the first Republican governor in the 20th century - Byrd made it impossible for him to elect a Republican senator.

I read it slowly, wanting to focus on it a bit. I did not criticize *The Post*, indeed I said perhaps *The Post* is right. What I didn't say but what was in my mind was that the more this assertion was accepted by Democrats, the more it would ease the shock of my leaving the Democratic Party.

In the short run it would hurt me with Republicans, but before the campaign was over, I felt I could make it a plus. I had confidence that if a Republican couldn't be elected, as *The Post* asserted, most Republicans would prefer me to a Democrat.

The second point *The Post* made was even more beneficial to me. The editorial said I didn't have to run as an Independent, rather, the editorial said the pledge "seems to us to be more of an excuse." Byrd, said *The Post,* could run as a Democrat simply by signing the oath required by the Democratic committee, and then, after election, ignore the pledge; *The Post* added that that's what most Southern Democratic senators do.

Here again, I did not criticize *The Post*. I said *The Post* had a point, and it did cross my mind. But, I asked myself, is that the kind of senator the Virginia people want.

I repeated, yes, I could have done what *The Post* recommended. But if I had done that, would I have been worthy of representing the people of Virginia in the United States Senate. How many newspapermen would sign a statement knowing they would later repudiate it?

I found *The Washington Post* editorial to be a valuable campaign tool. I carried it with me for weeks.

Chapter 7

✳✳✳✳

Naturally, I was tremendously interested as to what would be the reaction to my Declaration of Independence. I thought it would be 10 days, two weeks, perhaps a month before I could get a feel.

Ten days later *Time* magazine gave an appraisal, which, I acknowledged to myself, was probably the statewide consensus.

Time asserted:

"Byrd is the end of a dynasty of true conservatives," said one knowledgeable Senate aide. "His state is no longer conservative. Young Harry is out of step."

Time added:

"His chances are poor, and Byrd may well finish third in a three-way race."

-March 30, 1970

March 19, 1970 - *Norfolk Virginian Pilot* said, "One may doubt the wisdom, but scarcely the sincerity, of" Byrd's action. *The Pilot* said Byrd was "abandoning as near a sure victory as may be imagined in Virginia politics for a highly uncertain cause that invites double opposition."

Through the years while in the Senate I paid careful attention to the mail. My executive secretary, Audrey A. Jones, who, retired in 1986, after 39 years of close collaboration, made sure that I promptly saw every piece of mail which commented in any way on my speech to Virginians.

In five weeks, I received 6,000 letters, mostly handwritten. These were the letters to which I always paid the most attention. I felt that handwritten letters showed both conviction and commitment.

The response to my decision to run as an Independent was so favorable, I found it difficult to believe. I began to wonder if the bad letters were being withheld from me; but knowing Mrs. Jones, I knew that was not possible.

I received only a few letters from Democratic legislators, all unfavorable but not mean, more like friends expressing great disappointment. I got several dozen letters from persons on various local Democratic committees throughout the state. None of the letters defended the committee, nor said that I should sign the pledge. None was bitter but expressed sorrow that I needed to take the independent route.

With the letters running nearly 100-1 in my favor,

my staff wanted to issue a press release reporting on the favorable mail responses. I stopped them because I wanted to formulate my campaign strategy. I could see an opportunity, using the *Time* magazine piece and other published assessments to make the case as an underdog.

Although I have been in or around politics all of my life, I have yet to determine which is the stronger - the bandwagon vote or the underdog vote.

By that I mean are there more voters whose chief motivation is to be with the winner, or are there more who want to give the underdog a helping hand. Even today, I still don't know the answer.

But for me in 1970, it was not realistic to seek the bandwagon vote while running as an Independent. So my campaign strategy was to adopt the role of an underdog, even though my mail was running nearly 100-1 favorable.

The mail gave me tremendous confidence, as did the fact that very few letters or political leaders were defending the central committee. I kept hammering on the pledge requirement, and many citizens kept demanding that the committee reverse itself.

To my surprise, among those urging the Democratic State Central Committee to repeal the pledge requirement were the chairman of the Democratic Party, Congressman Watkins Abbitt, Attorney General Andrew Miller, Lieutenant Governor

Sargeant Reynolds and the just defeated Democratic nominee for Governor, William C. Battle.

The attitude of these leading Democrats further strengthened my position in refusing to sign the pledge.

I personally didn't care what the Central Committee did. If the committee took the pledge off, it vindicated my position; if the pledge requirement was left on, it kept the issue fully alive.

I reasoned either way would be to my benefit. The committee met in early May and voted to repeal the pledge requirement. The action came more than two weeks after the April 15 filing deadline.

Reaction among my Senate colleagues was muted. Many Democrats, I <u>had</u> to assume, were not happy but said little. Republicans, I <u>assumed</u>, were of two minds: Some felt it could mean an opportunity to attract me into the Republican Party, which quite a few had been encouraging for the past several years. Others, I surmised, were inclined to the view expressed by *The Washington Post* that I had made it impossible for a card-carrying Republican to be elected.

I didn't detect hostility from members of either party.

My Virginia colleague in the Senate was William Spong, a Democrat from Portsmouth. At 1:30 March 17, Bill was presiding over the Senate. I went to the presiding officer's desk and told him what I planned to do in a few hours. He was clearly stunned and could only say, "I hope you know what you are doing."

A week later, I was having lunch in the Senators dining room - where only Senators can go, and where we tend to speak bluntly to one another.

Senator James O. Eastland of Mississippi and I were having lunch together, just the two of us. He had been in the Senate for 28 years and was fourth in seniority. We were close friends. He brought up the subject of my campaign and asked who would be my campaign manager.

I told him I hadn't fully decided but was thinking of naming a newspaperman, the editor and general manager of one of my newspapers, a man with whom I had worked for 15 years.

Jim put down his knife and fork. He looked at me and said "You are a damn fool. First you are going to run for reelection as an Independent, and that's a fool thing to do. And now you are going to have a damn newspaperman who doesn't know anything about politics as your campaign manager."

"That's right, Jim, but Lathan Mims and I have worked together for 15 years. He knows how I think. He can make decisions without talking with me. And, most importantly, I know if he is doubtful about a course of action, he will take it up with me. He has solid judgment and I trust him completely."

As we finished lunch and were leaving the table, Jim, now friendly, said "I have been thinking about what you plan to do - I figure you want to run your own campaign."

"You are 100 percent correct," I replied, "I know exactly how I want it run."

As it turned out, that "damn newspaperman" ran the best campaign of the many in which I have been involved.

While my speech put Virginia politicians on the spot, Linwood Holton, the newly elected Republican Governor, had begun seeking an opponent for me as early as January, according to *The Washington Post*.

The New York Times reported on February 5 that Holton had urged Republican Congressman William Whitehurst of Norfolk to run against me; prior to that, according to news reports, he urged Congressman William Scott of Fairfax, and later Delegate Caldwell Butler of Roanoke, Holton's law partner, to run. One after another declined the opportunity.

Now that I had announced as an Independent, Holton was getting pressure from Republicans urging him to encourage me to seek the Republican nomination. His own view, I felt confident, would be to nominate a party member against me.

Speaking on NBC's "Today" show, Governor Holton made this comment:

"Senator Byrd is a strong individual. He has long paddled his own canoe . . . I personally think he made a mistake going the Independent course."

Holton added he would not urge Byrd to become a Republican. If Byrd wanted to become a Republican, it must be on the Republicans' own terms, Holton said.

The chairman of the Republican national committee, Rogers C. B. Morton, said "Byrd's Independent run suggests an excellent opportunity for an outstanding Republican to capture Byrd's seat."

Richard Nixon and I had been friends since he was elected to the Senate in 1950. We saw quite a bit of each other when he became Vice President. In 1969, soon after he became President, he invited me to the Oval Office and authorized me to contact him personally if there should be anything I wanted from his administration.

Richard M. Nixon

I gave him strong support in his efforts to end the Vietnam War. He talked with me about six or seven names he was considering for Supreme Court appointments.

We were friends who, despite different party affiliation, felt we could talk in confidence to each other. Whatever commitments he made to me, he kept. (That is more than I can say for some other Presidents).

With 1970 being the year I must run for reelection, the President talked with me several times about becoming a Republican. I listened but gave no indication of doing so. Key White House staff took a harder line in pressuring me.

As the date of the Republican State convention got nearer, I got a phone call from Bryce Harlow, a fine, able Nixon aide. I had worked with him on legislation from time to time.

Bryce phoned me one Friday morning (May or June) and asked me to join him for lunch at the White House. I sensed what he wanted to discuss and told him I had a luncheon commitment. He then asked if he could meet with me in my office; we set the time at 3 p.m.

After I became an Independent, I likened myself, in my own mind, to the man on his death bed to whom the priest was giving the last rites. When the priest asked "Do you denounce the devil and all his works," the sick one replied "In my condition, I don't denounce anyone."

Running against both political parties, I didn't want unnecessarily to make anyone mad.

So I listened to Bryce, said very little.

A real gentleman; he calmly outlined the many disadvantages facing an Independent, and then cited the advantages of becoming the Republican nominee.

Here again I said little but did point out that I had

been elected to public office seven times as a Democrat, had been treated very well by the Democratic Senate, had the best committee assignments, all of this despite the fact that I voted frequently with Republicans on legislation.

Bryce changed tactics a bit and then got to what he probably thought was his major point, his heaviest artillery.

"Senator," he said, "you probably want to know how we can guarantee you the Republican Senate nomination. The White House staff has thought a great deal about this and we have worked out a plan to assure a successful result.

"Here is what we will do. The President will have Governor Holton come to The White House, and the President and the Governor - the national leader and the state leader - will put their arms around you and say 'Harry's our man.' That will assure you the nomination."

Indeed it would; no doubt about that.

But I felt it also could severely damage my credibility and put me under obligation to Nixon, to Holton and to the Republican Party. It also would be inconsistent with what I told the Virginia people on March 17.

I kept my cool; I didn't comment on the proposal but thanked him for coming to see me. We had been talking two and a half hours.

Bryce, sensing that I was not enchanted with the

plan he presented, tried one more pitch: "Senator, the White House staff has given this Virginia election a tremendous amount of thought. The White House staff says you cannot win as an Independent."

At that point, I lost my cool.

I said "Bryce," and I remember these words well - "You tell the White House staff that I am willing to concede that the White House staff may know more than I do about every conceivable subject, except two - Virginia and Virginia politics. You tell the White House staff that I am going to run as an Independent, and I am going to be elected as an Independent."

Bryce kept <u>his</u> cool, and said "Senator, I can see you really mean it."

Chapter 8

✳✳✳✳

Events moved rapidly from April through June, as the following chronology shows.

APRIL - The chairman of the Republican Party, Warren French of Shenandoah County, called for all prospective candidates for the Senate to come forward. Among those responding were: Dr. Kenneth Haggerty of Arlington; Delegate Vincent Callahan of Fairfax; Walter Potter, newspaper publisher of Culpeper, and Horace E. Henderson of Virginia Beach, former Republican state chairman.

APRIL 16 - The Northern Neck Republican Association unanimously approved a resolution stating "The Republican Party should nominate Harry F. Byrd Jr. as its candidate for United States Senate, or publicly endorse his candidacy should he run as Independent. The association covers the counties of Lancaster, Northumberland, Richmond and Westmoreland.

APRIL 21 - Arlington County Republican

Committee asked Byrd to accept the Republican nomination, as did the Scott County Republican Committee in the Southwest.

In April, *The Associated Press* reported political winds still blowing strongly for Byrd as evidenced at the annual shadplanking event in Southside, a non-political event with heavy political overtones. It usually drew a crowd of 3,000 and was considered by politicians to be a "must attend" event.

MAY 25 - Republicans for Byrd Organization was formed by former Democratic Mayor Marshall Beverley of Alexandria. Delegate George Mason Green Jr., Republican, of Arlington, urged the Republican convention not to nominate a candidate, but rather to endorse Byrd.

State Senator Clive DuVal of Fairfax announced for the Democratic nomination. He said Byrd fails to serve needs of modern, rapidly growing state.

Earlier former Governor Godwin announced he would not run, as did state senator William B. Hopkins of Roanoke, Arthur Arundel, radio station owner of Fairfax, Congressman Thomas N. Downing of Newport News.

Governor Holton kept trying to find a Republican candidate, with Republican leader of House of Delegates Caldwell Butler prominently mentioned; he declined, again.

Northern Virginia Republican Congressman Joel

Broyhill publicly announced support for the movement to have Republican Convention endorse Byrd.

Republican women for Byrd formed June 22.

Democratic Chairman, Congressman Watkins Abbitt, introduced Byrd to a 3,500 crowd at the dedication of the Farmville Airport saying "Senator Byrd speaks our language."

JUNE 5 - "Republicans for Byrd" opened headquarters in Richmond; 34-member Finance Committee formed which included Lawrence Lewis, Jr.and J. S. Stetson Coleman, who was Holton's finance chairman the year before.

JUNE 8 - Statewide Republican Youth Group formed "Republican Youth for Byrd."

Amherst Republican Committee Chairman Vance S. Wilkins Jr. endorsed Byrd.

JUNE 12 - Republican State Senators George Barnes of Tazewell and Robert Burrus of Lynchburg endorse Byrd.

JUNE 15 - Henrico County Young Republicans endorsed Byrd.

JUNE 18 - Chairman Lynchburg Republican Committee endorsed Byrd.

JUNE 19 - Delegate Ray Garland of Roanoke announced for Republican nomination for Senate. Garland represented Roanoke, Salem and Roanoke County.

On June 15, I filed as an Independent candidate,

taking to the State Board of Elections a petition with the required signatures of qualified voters asking me to be a candidate. I wanted to make it clear to both the delegates to the Republican Convention convening June 26 and to potential voters in the July Democratic primary, that I was locked into an Independent run.

Chapter 9

✳✳✳✳

Between the three month period after my announcement as an Independent and the Republican convention on June 26, Republicans debated hotly as to whether the convention should or should not nominate a candidate against me.

Sentiment within the Republican party was divided. I had developed through the years many friends and supporters within the party. My voting record was generally acceptable to the average Republican.

GOP leaders, too, were split over whether to endorse my Independent candidacy for reelection or to nominate a Republican to run against me.

Governor Holton continued the leadership role in the effort to put forward a GOP contender. He later offered this explanation to Frank Atkinson, author of The Dynamic Dominion: "This has been my life - to build a two-party system in Virginia. And one year after we had first elected a state-wide candidate was not the time to throw up our hands and concede the election to an Independent."

Atkinson's book quoted Holton as saying "I like Harry Byrd personally, but his thinking and my thinking are different, particularly on this race issue (the busing of school children to achieve racial balance, a dominant issue in 1970)."

In a decisive banquet speech the night before the convention session, Holton urged delegates to field a candidate saying: "I have seen speculation in the papers that you will go home having done nothing. Frankly, I can't believe it. We are the biggest, strongest and the best party in Virginia....I can't believe we will do nothing. Doing nothing would be like having the biggest, shiniest fire engine and not taking it to the fire."

Republican Congressman, Joel Broyhill, who at that point had represented Northern Virginia in the U. S. House of Representatives for 18 years and was seeking reelection, was outspoken for me. He was leading the fight against the governor's position, and urged that no nomination be made. The Nixon White House sent a representative to back up Broyhill.

Congressman Broyhill, able and courageous, made a valiant effort on my behalf, taking on the full strength of the newly elected Republican governor. But in his zeal to help me, he made a statement on the eve of the convention that presented a problem for me. He said he "knew I would vote with the Republicans to organize the senate, if the Republican State Convention did not give him opposition."

I was in my office in Washington when Lathan Mims, who was in Richmond, telephoned me Broyhill's words.

I knew I had to act immediately - and I did so within minutes. Silence at this point, would, I thought, mislead the convention, and damage my Independent stance. I told the press that Joel was expressing only what he thought I would do. I said "I have made no commitments to anyone, except public commitments to all the people of Virginia." I regretted my necessity to damage Joel's efforts on my behalf. I said I would welcome convention endorsement, but could make no promises in order to get it.

When the roll was called, the governor's position prevailed by the vote of 644 - 420.

I regarded this as a victory for me, and for the Broyhill forces, because I had obtained the votes of 40% of the Republican activists. To me this meant that I would get a high percentage of the rank and file Republican voters in November.

The Republican nominee chosen by the convention was Ray Garland, a two-term member of the House of Delegates.

Garland's nomination was a major triumph for Governor Holton, whose leadership had been decisive in defeating the pro-Byrd effort.

Garland's nomination also went directly opposite to President Nixon's strategy, to quote The Dynamic Dominion, "for bringing about a massive restructuring in the South." The Atkinson book said the President "regarded Virginia's Senator Byrd as the key to it." Nixon, according to The Dynamic Dominion resented Holton's action and continued cool to Virginia's first Republican governor in the 20th century.

The Richmond Times-Dispatch warned editorially that Holton's triumph could be disastrous for the Republicans. Recalling his fire-engine analogy, the newspaper observed:

"At this point it appears that the only thing the Republicans can hope to get for their efforts in the Senate race is a battered and besmirched engine. Not only are they likely to lose the race, they're also likely to lose, temporarily at least, the goodwill of thousands of moderates and conservatives who had begun to regard the Republican Party as their new political home.

"Many moderates and conservatives had hoped the Virginia GOP would endorse, directly or indirectly, Sen. Harry F. Byrd Jr., a former Democrat who is seeking re-election as an Independent. Byrd has given Virginia responsible representation, and unless the mood of the state is deceptive, most Virginians probably approve the Senator's stands on major issues. Philosophically, Byrd certainly is closer to the Republican Party than he is to the Democratic Party he recently quit, and it is a fact that he has the respect - and will receive the support - of many of the conservative and moderate former Democrats who defected to the GOP last November and helped elect Gov. Holton."

The Democratic Primary to nominate a candidate for the U. S. Senate was held July 14, 1970. The three seeking the nomination were Milton Colvin, a professor at Washington & Lee University, State Senator Clive L. DuVal II of Fairfax County, and George C. Rawlings Jr., a former member of the House of Delegates from Fredericksburg.

My worry in regard to the Democratic primary was not who might win the nomination. My concern was what would be the total vote. If there was a heavy, or even normal, turnout, it would be a negative sign for me. I had felt that if the total vote for the three candidates combined did not exceed 300,000, that I could survive the November election. If the vote total exceeded that figure, I knew I would be in deep trouble.

When the votes were counted on the night of July 14, the total vote cast was 128,959. I found it difficult to believe such good news.

The small size of that vote said something loud and clear to the professional politicians: That guy Byrd may not be so dumb after all.

Seasoned politicians could read the political tea leaves: huge blocks of Democratic voters were staying out of the Democratic primary so as to vote for Byrd on

November 3rd.

Here is the official tally of the Democratic primary:

Rawlings	58,874
DuVal	58,174
Colvin	11,911

Rawlings was nominated by 700 votes and after the primary, the three Democrats in statewide office, Senator Spong, Lieutenant Governor Sargeant Reynolds and Attorney General Andrew Miller made a joint public statement promising their support of the Democratic nominee. The statement did not condemn me, but made clear the trio would maintain party regularity and vote against me.

I fully understood their position, and had no complaints. I thought they handled well a situation that clearly was awkward for them. They had in fact done me a favor by adding substance to my underdog strategy. I could now say - as I did many times - in my speeches, on radio and TV:

"The Governor is against me."

"The Lieutenant Governor is against me."

"The Attorney General is against me."

"My Virginia colleague in the Senate is against me."

"The only way I can be elected is if <u>you</u> will work for me and vote for me."

I was counting on the public's support for a fighting underdog.

With the Republican convention and the Democratic Primary having nominated candidates, and I, having filed as an Independent on June 15, a three-way race for the U. S. Senate was now underway. The total electorate would make the final decision on November 3.

In early August, Mills Godwin phoned me his support, and offered to take a key role in my campaign. On August 12, he made a public endorsement for me, and urged Democrats to stay in the party, but vote for Byrd. This was most welcome and very helpful.

The general election campaign for me did not really begin until September 10. I opened my campaign on that date at Manchester High School in Chesterfield County.

In the interim, there was much good news.

In terms of personal sentiment, I was greatly heartened to have the all-out support of two former colleagues in the Virginia legislature, Delegate Harrison Mann of Arlington and State Senator Robert Baldwin of Norfolk. Both opposed me vigorously when I ran for the Senate in 1966 against Armistead Boothe of Alexandria.

Bob Baldwin and I clashed when we were together in the State Senate. Hank Mann in 1966 was probably more outspoken against me than even was my opponent, Armistead Boothe. We barely were on speaking terms.

But after I had been in the Senate for 18 months or two years, Hank began to write me commending my voting record. By the time 1970 rolled around, we had become quite friendly, so much so that I asked if he would consider managing my campaign in Arlington County, one of the state's most populous counties. He agreed, and his help was invaluable in getting me the best vote I ever received from that difficult county.

Bob Baldwin became chairman of Virginians for Byrd in Norfolk.

It meant a lot to me to have the support and enthusiasm of two who opposed me so vigorously in 1966.

I worked to develop campaign structure in the various counties and cities to reflect a broad spectrum of the electorate.

Two examples dramatize this:

In the county with the largest population, Fairfax, I named as co-chairmen Frederick A. Babson Jr., Democrat, (and former chairman of the Board of Supervisors); Steven Hartwell, former chairman of the Mount Vernon District Republican Committee, and Beverley Mosby Coleman, former Finance Chairman of the Dranesville District Independent party.

In Norfolk, Virginia's largest city, on October 28, my campaign put together one of the largest political lunches ever held in the Hampton Roads area. *The Virginian-Pilot* the next morning called it an "astonishingly large, varied and enthusiastic audience". What really astonished the news media was the head table:

Former Governor Godwin, titular leader of the Democratic party; Stetson J.C Coleman, chief fundraiser for Governor Holton the previous year; and Leonard Strelitz, Henry Howell's number one fund raiser when Howell, a leader of liberal Democrats, ran for Governor the previous year.

Chapter 10

✳✳✳✳

With the three-way race a certainty, I began to put together the statewide campaign structure.

Lathan Mims, who had been acting as chairman of Virginians for Byrd, became Campaign Manager with the responsibility of developing an organization in each of the 134 counties and cities in the state, a Herculean task.

Delegate George N. McMath of the Eastern Shore county of Accomac became Chairman of Virginians for Byrd, the statewide organization. George, besides representing the Eastern Shore counties of Accomac and Northampton, was editor and publisher of *The Eastern Shore News*. A Democrat , he was popular with his colleagues in the Legislature. He had been elected to office and knew the rigors of campaigning.

As a steering committee with whom George and Lathan could consult, I was fortunate to have an outstanding one:

Former Governor Mills E. Godwin Jr., chairman. By common agreement, I believe, Mills was one of the greatest Governors Virginia had in this 20th century. Besides knowing the state so well, he was the titular head of the Democratic Party, and a keen political tactician.

Lewis Powell, former President of the American Bar Association, and a member of the State Board of Education, had been a leader of "Democrats for Eisenhower". His colleagues in that and other campaigns called him "the brain". (Later President Nixon appointed him to the U. S. Supreme Court).

In an earlier show of concern that I could not win as an Independent, Powell urged me to accept the Republican nomination. I responded that I

Supreme Court Justice Lewis F. Powell

had already told Virginians that I would seek reelection as an Independent. We talked at considerable length discussing the pros and cons of an Independent run. I walked with Lewis to his car, at which point he said, "You have convinced me that you have thought this thing through carefully and have a winning strategy." You can count on my support, he added.

Former Democratic State Senator from the City of Richmond, Fitzgerald Bemiss; former Democratic Speaker of the House of Delegates, E. Blackburn Moore; Ned Thomas, the chairman of the Arlington County Board of Supervisors, a Republican.

Those five were the steering committee.

J. Smith Ferebee of Richmond was Chairman of the Finance Committee, and Lewis Vaden of Chesterfield County, and a member of the Democratic Committee, was treasurer of Virginians for Byrd.

The campaign was in excellent hands.

Smith Ferebee was a dynamic and remarkable individual, in whom one could have complete confidence.

A native Virginian, he attended the Virginia Military Institute, went to Chicago in the depression era to earn a living. Later, he became the top producer for the Equitable Life Assurance Society, the huge insurance company.

In 1970, he took early retirement from Equitable to chair the committee to raise funds for my campaign. A formidable task it was, especially so when it must be without help from either political party.

That did not bother Smith. He liked challenges, and agreed to raise funds for me, before knowing whether I would run as a Democrat, Republican or Independent.

In early February he called a meeting of 30 persons to ask them to join him on the committee. We met at a motel near Richmond. Opening the meeting, I said frankly I did not know just how I would run, so said it is asking a lot of you to become a member of Smith's Committee, and give me in effect a blank check - not in financial but political terms.

I spoke about 20 minutes, then left and returned to Washington so the group could have a full and frank discussion without being encumbered by my presence.

Smith told me later that 26 of the 30 signed on; four wanted to wait until I determined how I would run; three of the four came aboard later.

Smith said, "Harry, your job is to attend to your Senate responsibilities; voting, office work, committee work, campaigning. We will do the fund raising. We will not interfere with you, and we prefer you not interfere with us."

That was music to my ears; I can't remember ever asking anyone for a contribution in any of my elections.

I did greatly disappoint Smith on at least one occasion.

Smith phoned me at my Senate office to say the mail brought two large checks - $5,000 each - the largest he had gotten. (We had put a limit of $5,000 from any one person or group).

When he told me the names of mother and daughter, I said to Smith I am sorry about this, but I must ask you to return both contributions. My problem is that I have taken an active interest in legislation they favored.

In actual fact, neither mother nor daughter would gain personally from the legislation which was enacted, but the daughter was trustee of a tax-exempt charitable foundation and she wanted a law to require tax-exempt organizations to pay a higher percentage of the funds to charity. It was a worthy cause and national in scope.

I asked Ferebee to return the contributions to forestall charges by political opponents that I received campaign funds from persons I helped with legislation, although it was for a good cause and easily explained. But a candidate can be damaged by being forced to explain something he had done.

J. Smith Ferebee

What follows next dramatizes the kind of person Smith Ferebee was, and should be of interest to every golfer.

On the day after the bombing of Pearl Harbor, he volunteered for the Navy, fully intending to become a flyer. But the Navy said he was too old to fly. Instead, Lieutenant Ferebee established and became the first executive officer of a naval flight instructor school at the Lewis School of Aeronautics in Lockport, Illinois.

In true Ferebee fashion, he made the Lockport

school the best of its type, and in his spare time he played golf and learned to fly. At 37, having proved himself, he was awarded his wings - the oldest naval officer with no flight experience prior to military service to receive them.

Soon after, he was transferred to the carrier Belleau Wood in the Pacific. When he was shot down on a mercy mission over Japan, he became the last naval officer to be taken prisoner in that country. After his release, with the rank of Commander, he spent several months in the hospital recovering from serious injuries. Doctors who treated him said he would never play golf again. But they didn't know J. Smith Ferebee.

To those who did, Ferebee's golf exploits were already legendary. At 31, he wagered $2,500 and half a Virginia estate that he could shoot 144 holes of golf between dawn and dusk. He did, and he didn't stop there. He next bet he could play 600 holes of golf in four days in eight different cities.

With a chartered DC-3, two pilots, a doctor, a nurse and an official scorekeeper waiting, Ferebee teed off in Los Angeles on September 25, 1938. During the four-day stint, he played 84 holes in Los Angeles, 81 in Phoenix, 72 in Kansas City, 72 in St. Louis, 75 in Milwaukee, 72 in Chicago, 72 in Philadelphia, and 72 in New York, finishing with a putt at the World's Fair. He averaged slightly over 85 strokes per round, exhausted 110 caddies, walked or ran 180 miles, lost 21 pounds . . . and collected $25,000.

But golf was not his only sport. In 1949 he shot 2400 rounds of skeet in four hours 18 minutes, breaking 85% of the targets. His exploits received nationwide publicity through articles in *Sports Ilustrated, Ford Times, Life, The New Yorker* and other popular magazines. And he was named to the Virginia Sports Hall of Fame.

With a can-do guy like Smith Ferebee raising the necessary funds, I knew the campaign budget would be balanced.

Chapter 11

✳✳✳✳

One of the most important issues to face the Congress in 1970 was President Nixon's proposal to reform the welfare system. I strongly favored welfare reform and looked forward to supporting the President's plan.

President Nixon submitted legislation drawn by one of his Democratic aides. It was referred to the Senate Finance Committee, of which I was a member. The committee spent most of the first half of the year 1970 holding public hearings on that important proposal.

Senator John J. Williams of Delaware, the senior Republican on the Finance Committee, took the lead role in analyzing that legislation. After spending many days and long hours questioning administration witnesses concerning the details of the welfare proposal, Senator Williams brought to light facts and figures that many senators found astonishing. I joined Senator

Williams in opposition to the proposed legislation.

The committee chairman, Russell Long of Louisiana, initially favorably disposed, as indeed was I, began to have doubts. The longer the committee hearings went on, the more skeptical Long became.

While no votes had been taken in the Finance Committee there appeared to be considerable opposition to the President's plan.

During August and early September, Mr. Nixon vacationed at the California White House, his personal home at San Clemente.

Mr. Nixon was worried as to the attitude of the Finance Committee and requested several members to meet with him at San Clemente so that he might get a better feel as to the details of the legislation. He wanted to know why Williams, Byrd and several others were so opposed, and why Long was so skeptical. He wanted a full discussion of his welfare legislation.

The President's plane, Air Force One, was put at the committee's disposal, but also taking along a number of White House aides whose presence Nixon needed in California.

From the committee there were the three ranking Democrats, Long of Louisiana, Abraham Ribicoff of Connecticut and Byrd of Virginia. On the Republican side there were Wallace Bennett of Utah, Paul Fannin of Arizona, and Jack Miller of Iowa.

We flew to California on September 2 and met

with President Nixon at his San Clemente home the following morning. Those of us opposed to the legislation had an opportunity to present our reasons.

Russell Long, as committee chairman, led the discussion, saying he was undecided as to how he would vote. In leading the discussion, Long, at one point said, "Mr. President, we are not concerned about the cost." I interrupted saying, "Mr. President, I don't like to interrupt Senator Long, but I want to make clear I am one senator who is _greatly_ concerned about the cost."

(Senator Long has told that story many times, even in recent years).

The legislation the President espoused was

Sen. Russell B. Long

complicated and there were many reasons to oppose it. But Senator Williams' interrogations established two facts which brought about the bill's defeat:

One, it would have doubled the number of people on welfare, and, two, it would have doubled the cost.

Senator Long became a strong opponent, and the bill went down in defeat.

In addition to enhancing my role in the death of a bad piece of legislation, the invitation to meet with the

President in California boosted my campaign. Historically, campaigns begin the first week in September. The President also invited the six Finance Committee members, including myself, to be his guests at a formal state dinner he was giving in San Diego for the President of Mexico.

So at the historical starting point of the campaign I had not one but two invitations from the Republican president. This greatly upset my Republican opponents in Virginia.

I began my campaign for reelection to the United States Senate on the night of Thursday, September 10.

That Byrd for Senate 8 p.m. rally was held in Chesterfield County at Manchester High School.

The weather was not cooperative. It rained most of the day and heavily between 6 and 7 p.m. I could see headlines the next day - small crowd attends Independent's rally, suggests Byrd in trouble.

In my mind's eye, I could see the pounding I would get from the news media: Few attend Independent's campaign rally.

At 7:30 the rain had lightened, but still drizzling; the school grounds were soaked. But cars were everywhere.

I began to feel better. The reception committee taking me from the car to a side door of the school seemed, I thought, more enthusiastic than warranted.

But when Kenneth Timmons, my campaign manager for Chesterfield County and the chairman of the night's rally, escorted me to the stage to a standing room only crowd, it was a sight that is still in my mind 28 years later. And when Ken whispered to me that there were several hundred more outside the hall for which loud speakers had been set up, it added frosting to the attendance cake.

Seated on the platform during the preliminaries, and observing the packed crowd - as well as the multitude of TV cameras and the horde of reporters, I lost my foreboding about the rain.

I became geared up, fired up.

The television cameras ground away, the crowd was so enthusiastic that I bore down hard on each of the various points that I wanted to get across. The frequent applause caused me to forget how hot the auditorium was that September night, the heat enhanced by the television lights.

The news accounts the next day said I spoke 32 minutes and was interrupted by applause 40 times.

When the speech was over, and after an hour of hand-shaking with those in the audience, my shirt, my suit and my body were as wet as if I had been submerged in a swimming pool.

For me, it was a night to be remembered - even to this day. What a wonderful way to start a campaign.

Lathan Mims, Jack Davis and I spent the night in nearby Petersburg where we were to start the next morning a campaign swing through four southside counties.

The reception I got from the people of Chesterfield County was so heart-warming, that I resolved that any subsequent campaigns of mine, would kick off at the same place, same time, same date.

For this campaign, the 9th congressional district was by far the most difficult for me. The 9th is in the mountainous Southwestern part of our state, beginning South of Roanoke and running to the Tennessee and Kentucky lines. It is home to the state's coal mines, the major coal mining counties being Wise, Tazewell, Russell, Buchanan and Dickinson.

Historically, in the 9th, there is no such thing as an Independent. The voters there are either Republican or Democrat. There is no middle ground. The 9th takes its politics very seriously, much more so than any of the now 11 congressional districts in Virginia.

From the date I announced as an Independent, I felt I could survive if I did not lose the 9th by more than 20,000-25,000 votes.

In making numerous phone calls to key political friends in the 9th, I soon found that not many desired "the pleasure of my company." Many said they were for me and wanted me elected and would help me quietly, but thought it better to keep my campaigning there to a minimum. I fully understood.

I needed to show activity, however, and made

some unnecessary and unproductive trips merely for the purpose of physically being in the 9th congressional district. I had support in both political parties but for the most part the vocal efforts on my behalf were from individual citizens, rather than from political leaders.

My basic strategy for the 9th was to get there from time to time with no particular purpose in mind, but to try to get some radio and newspaper coverage to show that I was not neglecting that beautiful part of our state.

I don't recall that we ever had a district-wide rally. As election day approached, I feared for the worst.

I was delighted when the votes were counted on November 3 and I had polled 30.7% of the total vote cast, against Rawlings 37.6%; Garland received 31.6%.

Thus I lost the 9th by approximately 6,000 votes - so much better than the heavy loss that I had expected. I ran third in a three-way race, but a close third.

Chapter 12

✳✳✳✳

The Senate that year did not adjourn until October 14. Thus, I had only two weeks for full-time campaigning.

Throughout my Senate career I had always taken the position that when the Senate was in session, my primary responsibility was to be there to vote. I had a 97% voting participation record, and even though the campaign was on, I felt an obligation to be at the Senate.

Both of my opponents kept demanding a debate. I replied that "I don't have time to educate Mr. Rawlings and Mr. Garland but that I would get them a seat in the Senate gallery and they could hear my speeches from there."

My campaign emphasized, too, that my record was well-known and that neither of them had a record that could justify debate.

After the Senate adjourned October 14, I was full-time on the campaign trail.

And, I began my campaign technique - a 12-ounce sirloin steak for breakfast. That way I could get by with little to eat - a glass of milk for lunch, and a light dinner. (I don't eat much if I have a speech to make, as was always the case at night).

My Democratic opponent called me the Republican from Winchester, as in the Senate I voted a great deal with the Republicans on legislative matters. My Republican opponent said I was too much of a Democrat, as I voted with the Democrats on procedural matters. I said both opponents were right.

Rawlings called Byrd "a do-nothing, vote-no, so-called senator". Garland attacked Byrd as a "system wrecker".

The Washington Post reported "a stinging attack" on Byrd by Holton and Garland campaigning together.

The Post reported that Holton and Garland said Byrd would bring a multi-party system to Virginia; Holton told audiences "an Independent candidate has about as much place in the Senate as a kangaroo."

In my speeches I emphasized that I am running on my Senate record saying "I could not change my record if I would; I would not change it if I could."

Throughout 1970, I kept two maxim in mind: one, don't shoot until you see the whites of opponents eyes; and, two, once a decision is made, "damn the torpedos, full steam ahead."

On October 20, Rogers C. B. Morton, the national chairman of the Republican Party, came to Virginia to seek support for Mr. Garland. Earlier on October 17 the Garland camp brought to Richmond, Senator Robert Packwood of Oregon. Senator Packwood, in his speeches in Virginia, said "We need a young leader like Mr. Garland. He's my kind of man."

In my speeches I quoted the senator from Oregon and said that one is justified in assuming that if elected my Republican opponent would vote similarly to Mr. Packwood.

Then I said "Let's look at Mr. Packwood's voting record":

• The Oregon senator is part of a hard-core group in the Senate determined to block any southerner nominated to the Supreme Court.

• He voted against President Nixon's Supreme Court nominees, both southerners.

• He voted against legislation for freedom of choice as to which school to attend.

• He voted in favor of forced busing of school children to achieve racial balance, taking them many miles from their home and from their neighborhood school.

• Despite President Nixon's plea, the Oregon senator voted against a bill aimed at controlling crime in the District of Columbia.

After citing these votes, and emphasizing that

Senator Packwood says my Republican opponent is "his kind of man." I emphasized that "I am not Packwood's kind of man," and that I voted against the way Packwood voted on all these important votes. So, I said, according to Senator Packwood the Virginia people have a clear cut choice: they can vote for "his kind of man," or they can vote for me.

The best I could judge the Packwood foray into Virginia was not especially successful, since Mr. Garland spent the next week denying he would vote the same way as Mr. Packwood. Having one's opponent on the defensive is my idea of a good campaign.

Beginning in October, and calling myself a "forward looking conservative," I called Rawlings, without mentioning his name, "an extreme liberal." I totally ignored Garland. I spoke in the singular, "My opponent, an extreme liberal."

To me, it was obvious that Rawlings was the only threat to my reelection. He had virtually the total black vote in his corner, plus the strong support of labor union leaders and the liberal Democrats. Garland was not a factor.

I was cheered, too, by the formation of a group of construction workers - "Hard Hats for Harry".

By late in the campaign, many members of the legislature began to take sides:

21 Democrats endorsed Rawlings

30 Republicans endorsed Garland

30 members endorsed Byrd - 28 Democrats, 1 Republican and 1 Independent.

In late October, I campaigned in five counties around Roanoke and Lynchburg, beginning in the early morning and ending about 9 o'clock that night.

When I arrived at my motel, Lathan Mims was awaiting me with the news that Vice President Spiro Agnew had called and wanted to talk with me. I returned the call and the phone at the other end was answered by Bryce Harlow. One of President Nixon's top aides, he was traveling with the Vice President.

Bryce said "Senator, a great American is calling you - Vice President Agnew."

When Ted Agnew got on the phone, he said "Senator, I wanted to give you a firsthand report on what happened today. I was campaigning for Republican candidates in North Carolina and at the airport as I was preparing to leave the state, the press queried me and one of the questions was: Since you have been supporting all of the Republican candidates in North Carolina, do you support the Republican candidate for the Senate in Virginia? Ted said "Senator, of course I had to say yes, in order to keep my credibility."

I was both tired and hungry, not having had either lunch or dinner. My reply to Agnew was blunt: "Ted, that's a lot of bunk. And you know it. You were in New York last week and you did not endorse the Republican Senate nominee. In fact, you endorsed the conservative party nominee, James Buckley. I am glad you endorsed Buckley and hope he wins. But for you to tell me you had to endorse my opponent to keep your credibility, that is a lot of bunk."

"Senator," Ted said, "I promise you I will not mention the Virginia campaign again."

I hung up. It was a brief conversation.

The next morning the president's press secretary told the news media that Agnew was speaking only for himself, he was not speaking for President Nixon.

Throughout the campaign, I felt confident I would win. I was not seeking a majority as I thought that to be impossible. I did feel I had rock-bottom support of 43 or 44 or maybe 45 percent of the total vote, which in a three-way race would be a winner.

I knew the black vote, which was to total 142,000, was always monolithic, with the Democratic candidate receiving more than 90 percent (it made up nearly one-half of Rawlings total.)

The labor union leaders gave Rawlings' strong support, but the union members gave me a plurality - without which I couldn't have won such a smashing victory.

But feeling certain that virtually the entire black vote would be cast for my Democratic opponent, and knowing that the union leaders were doing everything possible for Rawlings, I took nothing for granted.

On the Friday before the election, I began early

that morning campaigning in the Richmond area, with the last event being a reception-rally given me by the Greek-American community in Richmond. It ended after midnight and Jack Davis, who was driving, and I headed for Winchester and a 7 a.m. breakfast given for me by my hometown friends.

En route is a large truck stop between Richmond and Fredericksburg. As we approached that area, I told Jack the election could be decided by only a few votes so, I wanted to shake hands with every trucker there.

I did just that. It was crowded and took quite a while. We got back on the road to Winchester about 2 a.m. and it was after 3 a.m. when we reached Winchester.

En route, Jack and I compared notes. We found that only a few of the truckers were Virginians - most were from New York, New Jersey, South Carolina, Georgia and Florida.

I told Jack, no more truck stops.

Chapter 13

As an abstract of my views on the issues in the campaign, and of my style of campaigning, I offer excerpts from my speeches and from press reports.

• "I shall support the President, Democrat or Republican, when I believe him to be right - and I shall oppose the President, Democratic or Republican, when I believe him to be wrong."

• "A lot of lawlessness goes back to Supreme Court decisions. The Court is too far to the left, needs to be brought back to center."

• "It is time to take the handcuffs off the police and put them where they belong . . . on the criminal."

• "All of us have a deep obligation to help the physically and mentally handicapped, but I don't understand programs that would take taxes from hardworking wage earners to give to able-bodied who refuse to work."

• "Taxes are paid in the sweat of every man who labors.

• "I shall seek to vote the conscience of Virginia."

• "My campaign is a crusade for good government."

• "We must balance the federal budget. We had have too many years of deficit spending."

• "We must maintain a balance between the anti-pollution effort and economic development needed to provide jobs for our young people."

From the Press:

Charles McDowell in the Richmond Times-Dispatch, March 10, 1970

WASHINGTON - When the Virginia General Assembly has gone home and its reverberations have subsided, and when the flu weather has yielded to real springtime, Sen. Harry Flood Byrd Jr. will make an announcement to his fellow Virginians.

It will not be elaborate or strung out. It will be phrased in the simple declarative sentences, short and punchy, which probably have done more to give Byrd a clear, firm "image" than a clutch of Madison Avenue copywriters might have done on long-term contract.

Slick ghostwriters will not be needed. Harry Byrd seems to have been born knowing the uses of simplicity and clarity, the active voice, and calculated redundancy in impressing a brand name on the minds of the public . . . .

A Richmond advertising agency is preparing Byrd campaign material. It emphasizes words and concepts like "independence" and "integrity," and the message is that this man of integrity is independent to the degree that he is almost above partisan politics.

The issues will be simple and clear, and Byrd's positions will be strong, and the sentences will be short with the verbs in the active voice. If the copy isn't written that way, the editor-candidate will make it that way.

The Washington Post, November 1:

"All the keys press together turn out the principal theme of the Byrd campaign: "You know where he stands."

Key phrases from his March 17 statement and from the one which Byrd opened his campaign September 10, are becoming household words, for they have been repeated by the candidate at every stop.

The result is familiarity, the softness and comfort of old clothes. They know indeed what Senator Byrd stands for.

It is that quality of constancy that has led some political observers to predict Byrd's election "because he is a certain commodity in uncertain times.

"Byrd goes around the state with his strong handshake, always smiling, his high-pitched laugh, saying the same thing in speeches and being gracious, polite and gentlemanly."

The Associated Press - November 1, (Sunday before election):

Inflation and the cost of living, crime in the streets, campus unrest, busing of school children, the Far East, the Middle East?

Which are the principal issues in Virginia's unique three-way Senate race?

All are doubtless factors to more of less degree.

But the principal issue is a matter of political philosophy - the conservative philosophy of the candidate whose stance in this election makes the race unique, Sen. Harry F. Byrd Jr. running as an Independent in the role of favorite.

Daily, George C. Rawlings Jr., the liberal Democratic candidate, and Ray L. Garland, the moderate-conservative Nixon-Holton type of Republican, shoot at Byrd from both sides.

He's part of the Republican apparatus in Washington that doesn't know what to do about the economy, the Rawlings camp argues, adding that he represents the vested interests and not the best interests of the broad mass of Virginians.

Byrd is a do-nothing senator, Garland contends, and hasn't come through as consistently for the Nixon programs as Garland would do if elected. And he says Byrd talks about economy and then votes to override a presidential veto on an overly-expensive appropriations bill. As for the issue - Byrd is the issue for Garland and Rawlings and much of their recent campaign efforts have been devoted to trying to persuade the undecided voter that each has the only chance to beat Byrd and the other one doesn't. Instead of standing eyeball-to-eyeball across major party lines and shooting at one another, Garland and Rawlings have had to keep firing away at the Independent out on the flanks who has risen above any debate confrontations with his opponents and never mentions them by name in his speeches.

On the hard issues - inflation, crime, busing and foreign affairs - the candidates differ mainly in degree. But Byrd's stance on all of them is known and his position seems well identified with the problems that cry out for solution.

Byrd blames the main reason for inflation and soaring costs on deficit spending by the Congress for nonvital programs.

Norfolk-Virginian-Pilot, Saturday, October 31

RICHMOND - Promising to "vote the conscience of Virginia" in the Senate, Sen. Harry F. Byrd Jr. brought the house down and the crowd to its feet Friday.

Byrd campaigned all day in the streets and stores of downtown Richmond.

He bubbled with confidence and even appeared to soften his attack of the last few days on his Democratic opponent, George C. Rawlings Jr.

Byrd's major appearance was at a rally in the John Marshall Hotel, with Lewis F. Powell Jr., Mills E. Godwin Jr. and Kenneth Smith also speaking. Powell is a nationally prominent lawyer, Godwin the last governor of Virginia, and Smith a 14-year-old high school freshman, chairman of Teen-agers for Byrd.

The Byrd speech was generally a combination of all the same points the senator has been making for months across the state.

But one standard line was missing. That was the one about taking "the handcuffs off the police and putting them back where they belong - on the criminals."

It always gets applause for Byrd, but he left it out Friday in Richmond. Young Smith, speaking earlier with the temerity older politicians wouldn't muster, stole the senator's line in his own speech. It got applause for him, too.

In fact, young Smith almost was a show stealer. He was applauded six times, in a five-minute speech, including one burst of applause when he complained that he was unable to see over the lectern from which he was speaking.

The enthusiastic crowd of about 400 Richmonders was in an applauding mood. The Byrd speech, which drew 14 interruptions for applause in Norfolk Wednesday, got 17 in Richmond - even with the handcuffs off.

Mostly, the two audiences - Norfolk and Richmond - even applauded in the same places. One exception was the silence of the prosperously dressed Richmonders' hearing Byrd's expectant pause after the line, "Taxes are paid in the sweat of every man who labors."

But the Richmond audience rose with a roar and applause to the line that follows, "I shall seek to vote the conscience of Virginia."

Republican opponent Ray Garland was almost ignored in the Charlottesville and subsequent speeches. By Friday, polls had been made public that showed Byrd well ahead and Garland far behind with still a large "undecided" vote.

The Associated Press, October 31 (Reporting on my last campaign speech):

BERRYVILLE (AP) - Sen. Harry F. Byrd Jr., winding up his campaign for re-election as an independent, said Saturday he is "fighting for balance" in the government of the United States.

"I want to see balance in the budget of the U. S. government," Byrd said in a speech during a tour of the Shenandoah Valley. "We have had too many years of deficit spending."

Byrd said he wanted, too, "to see balance in the Supreme Court. For too many years now, the court has leaned too far to the left. It needs to be brought back to a more moderate position."

The senator said because of "this need for balance," he supported all of President Nixon's nominees to the court, "including the two strict constructionists rejected by a hard core of Senate liberals."

He added he wanted "to see balance" among the executive, the legislative and the judicial branches of government.

Byrd said the judiciary "has become too powerful. Federal judges are ignoring the express will" of the Congress and the President.

He added he planned to sponsor a constitutional amendment to put a limit on the term of office of these judges, who now serve for life.

"I also want to see a balance between the rights of the victims of crime and the rights of those accused of crime," Byrd said.

"Recent federal court decisions, particularly decisions by the Supreme Court, have over-emphasized the rights of the accused at the expense of the rights of law abiding citizens."

Turning to the subject of pollution, Byrd said "We need clean water and air," and added he has supported all major environmental legislation.

"At the same time," he said, "we also need economic development to provide job opportunities for the young men and women graduating from our schools and colleges."

Asserting the federal government has "too much power," Byrd called for a balance between the authority of the federal government, on the one hand, and the rights of the states and the individual citizens, on the other.

"I shall fight for the rights of the individual citizen, his community and his state, against the overwhelming power of the federal government," the senator said, adding he embraced and supported "a philosophy of forward-looking conservatism."

Byrd's campaign day began at a "welcome home" breakfast in Winchester that drew a standing-room only crowd of 500.

Chapter 14

As every reader can well imagine, that night of November 3, 1970 was, for me, the night of a lifetime. First returns from the voting began to come in about 8 p.m. The results were favorable right from the beginning - but continually got better. When it appeared I might get a majority of the vote - more than the combined total of my two opponents - I found it difficult to believe.

My first thoughts were those of deep appreciation to the people of Virginia. The people had given me a "blank check," authorizing me to vote as I felt was best for the nation without regard to political party. Never before in the history of the United States Senate had anyone received more votes than the nominees of both the major parties combined, and only once before (Norris of Nebraska, 1936) had anyone been elected against opposition from both major parties.

Here are the final results:

Byrd (Ind.)   506,237 54%
Garland (Rep.)   147,765 15%
Rawlings (Dem.)   294,582 31%

Byrd carried 121 of the 134 counties and cities in Virginia.

Rawlings carried 10.

Garland carried only Dickinson, Scott and Carroll all in the southwest part of the state.

In Norfolk, the state's most populous city, Rawlings won by less than 500 votes:

Rawlings   20,867
Byrd   20,371
Garland   4,683

Rawlings carried only three cities, Galax and Norton in the Southwest and Norfolk.

Garland lost every city, including his home city of Roanoke.

Byrd carried nine of the 10 congressional districts, losing only the 9th where he ran behind both Rawlings and Garland.

Former Governor Godwin made the following statement:

"This has been a truly great day for Virginia. Senator Byrd has scored a landslide victory. It emphasizes again the philosophy which made this nation great and which Virginia clearly desires to preserve."

In other comments on election night, I noted what an "unusual and amazing" campaign it was, starting from "scratch", and mainly by those who had not been active in politics before; it was a team effort."

I noted that my young supporters had formed Byrd chapters on 23 college campuses, won most of the mock elections, and played a very important part in the campaign, as did the women.

I urged women to continue to involve themselves in politics because "they can bring an idealism to government that government badly needs."

Here is my statement as reported by the Associated Press:

WINCHESTER (AP) - Sen. Harry F. Byrd Jr. Tuesday night hailed his decisive reelection as an independent as proof that Virginians "value principles of government above political partisanship."

In a statement, Byrd said:

"I am deeply grateful to the people of Virginia for their tremendous vote of confidence.

"I am especially pleased that this vote came from every section of our Commonwealth, and from every political segment: Democrats, Republicans and Independents.

"I regard this not as a personal victory, but rather do I regard it as a victory for a sound philosophy of government.

"The people of Virginia have shown the nation that they value principles of government above political partisanship - and at the same time they have made political history.

"Last March I refused to take an oath to a political party. Tonight I do take an oath - an oath to all the people of Virginia.

"To every Virginian, I pledge that I shall continue to strive to represent the conscience of our great state."

Chapter 15

✳✳✳✳

Here are excerpts from some post-election editorials:

The Richmond News Leader, Nov. 4 - More Virginians went to the polls than in any off-year election in the state's history. The total vote was 948,584, of which Byrd received 506,237.

Washington Star, Nov. 4 -Byrd's majority as an Independent in a three-way race will be recorded as a personal triumph and a historic one. He won impressively without the Democratic Party that his father dominated for four decades.

Roanoke World-News, Nov. 4 - U. S. Senator Harry F. Byrd Jr. has won reelection easily, giving him a victory unprecedented in Virginia politics.

His win yesterday was immediately interpreted . . . as meaning the state Democratic Party must become more conservative.

There was also the feeling that Byrd can take over

a Democratic leadership role if he wants it.

He carried all the state's 10 congressional districts except one .....

The victory was widely interpreted as a personal victory for Byrd and the conservative philosophy he has espoused.

Richmond Times-Dispatch, Nov. 4 - By their overwhelming endorsement of Independent Senator Harry F. Byrd Jr., voters assured Virginia of able and responsible representation in the U.S. Senate for the next six years ... The Senate race, clearly showed that to Virginia voters principles are more important than party labels.

The Washington Post, Nov. 5 - The stunning victory by Senator Byrd in his reelection bid left dismayed Republican and Democratic leaders in Virginia groping for reasons and remedies.

The Clarke Courier, Nov. 5 - It took a great deal of fortitude, a daring gamble, thought and honesty for Byrd to risk his office by breaking away from the Democratic party.

The Roanoke Times, Nov. 5 - For Harry F. Byrd Jr. - a man without a party, but a man with strong convictions, a good name and rock-like integrity, Tuesday's Senate election was an astonishing victory. Senator Byrd won in a way that once had seemed inconceivable: capturing a solid majority of votes and in a big turnout election.

New Orleans Times-Picayune, Nov. 8 - One of the most remarkable victories was the reelection of Senator Harry F. Byrd Jr. of Virginia who had renounced his life-long Democratic label to run as an Independent.

After the stunning triumph over the Democratic and Republican candidates, Senator Byrd is the number one man politically in the Old Dominion, and he apparently can write his own political ticket for the future.

On December 31, *The Associated Press* ranked Byrd's Independent campaign and land-slide victory as the top Virginia news story of 1970.

Chapter 16

✳✳✳✳

The new congress convened in January 1971, two months after Virginia voters gave me a mandate to vote as I deemed best. For the past five years I had voted with the Democrats on Senate organizational matters, and had received my committee assignments - Finance and Armed Services - from them. While many friends urged me to align with the Republicans, I saw little reason to change what I had been doing for five years, namely, voting with the Democrats on procedural matters and voting independently on legislation.

Democratic Senator Fred Harris of Oklahoma led an effort to deny me seats on Finance and Armed Services, the two committees I considered the most important in the Senate. Mike Mansfield of Montana, the Senate Democratic Leader, publicly assured me there would be no change in my committee assignments.

Of the 57 Democrats, the Harris effort had the support of only five. Thus, I became one of only three colleagues (the others being John Stennis of Mississippi and William Fulbright of Arkansas) to be accorded the privilege of serving on two of the top four committees: Finance, Armed Services, Appropriations and Foreign Relations. The Harris effort to punish me for running as an Independent was overwhelmingly defeated.

I found my role as an Independent increasingly desirable. When I ran for reelection in 1976, I again ran as an Independent and became the only person in Senate history to be twice so elected. I did not seek re-election in 1982, and left the Senate in January 1983, after 36 years in elected public office.

Through the years, I have been asked my own assessment of the impact of my 1970 decision. In Virginia, the magnitude of my victory accelerated the trend away from strict party line voting. The Republicans benefitted. My victory in 1970 made it easier for conservatives like Mills Godwin to move from the increasingly liberal Democratic Party into the Republican Party. In 1973 Godwin was again elected Governor, this time running as a Republican. I was told by Senate colleagues that my victory had an impact, too, in other Southern states.

I end this book by trying to envision whether an Independent candidate could win the Presidency, as the President is elected by the electoral college, not by popular vote. I think it could be done, but various elements must come into play simultaneously.

First, the two political parties must both be weak. That situation exists today. The astute Charles Bartlett, author of *Coleman/Bartlett's Washington Focus*, put it best. He wrote in his mid-June 1998 report that President Clinton and his Vice President, Albert Gore, "draw their pay these days from doing little more than flying around the country, making political hay and cosmetic reaches for popular favor. There is no real substance, at this point, in the Clinton administration."

That lack of substance is likely to continue; nor is there effective Democratic leadership in the Congress. Vice President Gore probably will get the Democratic presidential nomination in 2000 but I think the odds are against his election.

The Republican Party is virtually leaderless. The Speaker of the House of Representatives, Newt Gingrich, did a magnificent job for his party when he captained the successful team effort four years ago to elect a Republican congress. He more than any other individual deserves the credit.

But the Newt Gingrich of 1998 is not the Newt Gingrich of 1994. After winning a great victory, he ignored a truism I learned as a 10-year-old from my grandfather: "The time of greatest victory is the time of greatest danger." If Newt knows where he stands on the various issues, he has not made that clear to many Americans.

The American people deserve better from both

political parties. There is adequate time for a magnetic Independent leader to emerge along with a burning issue that neither major party candidate wishes to tackle.

In the last presidential election, for example, Republican candidate Senator Dole found it so politically comfortable to tend the brush fires that he never got to the big ones.

As a newspaper editor covering the Republican convention in Philadelphia in 1940, I watched Wendell Willkie, a public utility executive with no political experience, capture by sheer personality the presidential nomination against the two front runners, Governor Tom Dewey of New York and Senator Robert Taft of Ohio.

Yes, as difficult as it would be, I can envision an individual running successfully as an Independent when both political parties are weak, and the other elements are in place: a magnetic personality, adequate financing, a compelling issue, and the courage to stay on a strategic course.